REALLY RURAL

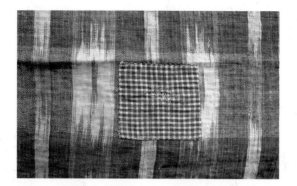

REALLY RURAL

AUTHENTIC FRENCH COUNTRY INTERIORS

MARIE-FRANCE BOYER

WITH 200 ILLUSTRATIONS,

173 IN COLOR

THAMES AND HUDSON

FOR SARA.

IN MEMORY OF MATHURINE TRIBROCHE AND OF MARIANNE CAIN;

AND OF LA CONCHE TO ESCLAVOLLES,

KERGONAN TO PEN ARLAND.

DESIGNED BY MICHAEL TIGHE

Translated from the French by John and Véronique Wood

©1997 Thames and Hudson Ltd, London
Published in France in 1997 by Thames & Hudson SARL Paris as *Les Intérieurs du Monde Rural*
English translation ©1997 Thames and Hudson Ltd, London

First published in the United States of America in 1997 by Thames and Hudson Inc., 500 Fifth Avenue, New York, New York 10110
Library of Congress Catalog Card Number 97-60246
ISBN 0-500-01799-9

Printed and bound in Hong Kong by South Sea International

Page 1: bread baskets, Auvergne, south-central France, woven from rye straw and bramble.
Page 2: interior of timber-framed house, Landes, south-west France. *Title-page:* flame-patterned linen cloth,
Poitou, west-central France. *Pages 4–5:* cottage with schist roof and vegetable garden.
Background, this page: inside a barn, Aveyron, in the south.
Contents: picture of the Sacred Heart, Ushant, Brittany; bedroom, Loubaresse, Massif Central;
eighteenth-century style bed, Landes; living room, Landes; kitchen, Auvergne.

CONTENTS

Perhaps we cannot talk about an 'aesthetic' in discussing rural domestic interiors that have been altered over the years by successive generations. Yet these rooms for communal living or sleeping – or both – deserve our attention for their complete authenticity and even a certain sensuous appeal. Since the 1980s we have been saturated with the cult of 'interior design' and the excesses of modern consumerism; here we find only the barest essentials, a feeling that life is hard, sometimes poignant in its simplicity, but at the same time suggesting a great strength of values. There are many lessons to be learned from these homes that belong to a previous age.

The rural way of life reached its peak between the end of the eighteenth and the middle of the nineteenth century. The advent of the railway started a massive exodus from the countryside. Schooling and military service opened up a world which had

INTRODUCTION

been closed on itself. Creativity flourished with the economic expansion of the rural areas, and this was the golden age of furniture-making, pottery, basketwork – the arts and crafts of everyday life. During the eighteenth century 85 per cent of the French population lived in the country; by 1850 it was only 75 per cent, by 1914 no more than 50 per cent, falling to 33 per cent by 1940 and 10 per cent by 1980.

Today the agricultural way of life is in complete decline, and it was only by going to the remotest regions and finding the oldest inhabitants that we discovered authentic rural interiors. In the households of the generation immediately preceding ours, the new has not yet completely supplanted the old, and the mixture of materials, forms and functions is still clearly rural as distinct from urban, but it is a hybrid style, a 'transitional' style. It is therefore predominantly people of the generations born

before 1920 and 1940 who are presented in this book; the interiors of the generations that came after them have a style that is less characteristically rural.

Anyone growing up just after the Second World War, and even in the 1960s, who was lucky enough to spend summer holidays in the French countryside will remember going to the farm for milk. If you arrived too early, carrying your little tin milkcan, the farmer's wife would still be in the cowshed. You would slip into its warmth with its sounds of rustling straw and ruminants' mouths, and its distinctive smell. Standing in the shadows thrown by the bare electric light bulb, you waited until the farmer's wife returned to the *salle* (the living room). Putting her heavy metal basin on to the smooth, unpolished table top, surrounded by a small swarm of flies, she would ladle out the frothing milk, lapping and splashing. Absorbing the atmosphere of the place, you looked around and saw the box-bed overflowing with crumpled, multicoloured bedding, the glowing embers and grey ash of the hearth, the cats and the dogs, and the old people, seemingly ancient, sometimes confined to bed and lying back to the wall. The hens would wander in and out, over the earth floor which was full of bumps and hollows. For a child, each trip for the milk was a special treat – a journey to another and fascinating world. It was only much later that you learned to see with different eyes this other world in which people ate and slept, were born and died.

Page 9: the stove – fuelled by wood, gas or coal – is at the heart of family life. In the Massif du Pelvoux, in the Hautes-Alpes, it has to be lit as early as August. *Opposite above*: sleeping arrangements, Brittany, 1910; *below*: child's box-bed under the staircase, in the Auvergne.

11

From the beginning of the twentieth century there was a series of changes that affected this way of life. In 1900, candles and oil lamps were still the only source of artificial lighting. The living quarters were kept warm by the heat from the animals – in the Haute-Savoie, for instance, the cowshed was often only separated from the *salle* by the gutter from the dungheap. Between 1920 and 1930, however, wood-fuelled stoves were installed in the *salle* beneath a mantelshelf. The major break with tradition occurred in 1940 with the fairy godmother electricity and her magic light

bulbs. Electricity also opened up the way for radiators, chain saws, milking machines,

freezers and other appliances. The electricity meter arrived – a conspicuous blemish,

still an eyesore today. With the arrival of gas and mains water supplies between 1950

and 1960, pipes, water heaters and gas cylinders began to disfigure the beautiful

roughcast plasterwork, wooden beams and partitions. The old stoneware, earthen-

ware and copper utensils fell out of use, and refrigeration replaced salt in the

preservation of food, while materials and techniques for carrying, preparing and

cooking it also changed. The old skills and artefacts disappeared: countrymen before

1914, and even up to 1930, knew how to quarry stone to build their own houses, and

worked in wood, straw and wickerwork in any time they had to spare from working the land. The imagination and ritual intimately linked with these ancient arts has been lost, and so has the individuality of objects made by people who brought their own experience of nature and life to their craft. Raw materials are now brought in from elsewhere. One 'goes into town', orders and buys. It is all so much easier. The age of consumerism has arrived. Now it is only the old who still know the names and uses of those everyday objects which have become relics of the past, the very same objects that we now collect. Who in France today knows what is meant by the terms *fromager* (a cheese strainer), *chopine* (a cider measure), *jatte* (a batter measure), *potager* (a stove filled with embers from the fire to keep food hot) or *kibrik* (a wicker basket from the Dordogne)? We reappropriate shapes and forms which, taken out of context, lose much of their significance. Those ancient houses where the old ways are still followed help us to understand the interaction between the region, its geography, climate, architecture, furniture and everyday objects – the table matched to the width of the window, the earthenware dish that seems made for the table, the bench that fits the foot of the bed, the clock and the bed together exactly fitting the width of the wall. There is a relationship between stone walls, schist roofs and the Auvergne landscape; between clay pitcher and spring, cooking pot and smoke-blackened granite hearth, between rush baskets and the neighbouring countryside.

Ethnologists have known this for a long time. It is now more than a century since Swedish peasant homes were reconstructed at the Skansen Museum in Stockholm in 1891. In France, it was not until 1970, thanks to the enthusiasm of Georges Rivière, that the first Ecomuseums were set up. But today these old country interiors have an even greater relevance now that our own domestic arrangements are having to adapt to the new computer and hi-fi equipment with its modern materials, forms and colours. In the past these country households were the setting for unchanging social and religious rituals, but, swept along with the rest of the world by the changes of modern life, they are conforming to different patterns. Wipe-clean table-cloths, machine-made lace and nylon curtains reflect the current taste of the householders, who all watch the same television channel at the same time of day. During the past fifty years, the rural interior has lost some of its beauty, but its style remains an essential point of reference, still very different from that other hybrid which seems to claim kinship with it: the peasant house converted into a second home. It will no doubt take several generations, much thought and extreme sophistication to reconcile once again those two diametrically opposed environments – the domestic interior and the untamed world of nature that surrounds it.

Preceding double page: in the Cantal in the Auvergne, stocks of firewood are ready before the onset of autumn, well before the time when plants have to be brought in from the cold. *Opposite*: an ivory-coloured Breton dresser looks like a little altar from a chapel. Coloured glass balls from the local religious festivals known as Pardons, the boat, the flowers under the glass dome and the faïence bowls (made of earthenware with an opaque glaze) are reminders of seafaring ancestors, friends, God and the saints.

14

EVERYDAY OBJECTS

Patching and darning

In isolated parts of the countryside everyone used to know how to mend. Like knitting and basket weaving, this was usually done beside the fire on winter evenings. Patches – round, rectangular or irregular in shape – were stitched to the garment using a flat, overcast or edge-to-edge seam. Cloth had to be chosen that was neither too strong nor too flimsy. *Opposite: centre left*: a flat seam; *top left*: a darn using needle and thread to strengthen or repair the original fabric by drawing threads at right angles, biased or even in tulle stitch – a skilled technique, in contrast to the rough and ready method called *pédasse* for repairing a tear with 'mule tooth' stitch – in this instance on a jute potato sack *(right)*. Today these mending skills are all but forgotten. They are moving in their simple artistry – recalling old-fashioned reading primers with their unexpected variety of textures, colours and patterns.

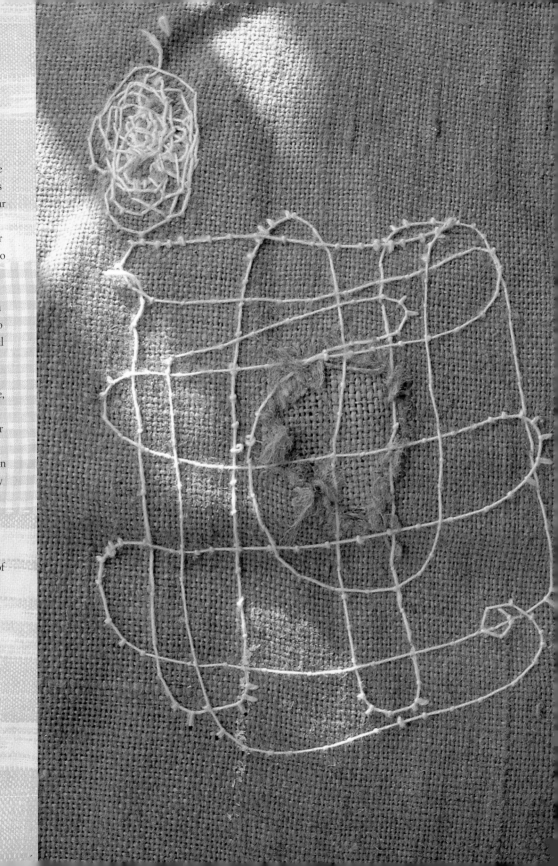

It is about a ten-hour drive from Paris to the southern Auvergne, or to the Hautes-Alpes on the Italian frontier halfway between Grenoble and Nice. Here the traveller enters remote and mountainous landscapes. In the Cantal in the Auvergne, the schist roofing of the houses reaches down so low that it becomes part of the lichened rocks. The granite walls, robust and foursquare, display their natural material to perfection; the slightest modern addition disfigures them unmercifully. Breeze-blocks, raw new plasterwork, wire fencing and corrugated iron are indications of poverty and isolation defacing one of the most extraordinary landscapes in France.

Noël's farm and the farm owned by the brothers Marcel and Jean (all three men are bachelors) consist of groups of buildings and are set in small hamlets. In these two farms, as in the Berthalons' farm near Briançon in the Hautes-Alpes, the living area,

OLD ROOTS

the focus of domestic life, takes up only a small space. Animals are still considered the most important members of the household. All three farmhouses have the same allocation of space, shared out between the *salle* – the communal living room – and the bedroom. You are hardly over the threshold and into the entrance – itself an integral part of the decor – before you are assailed by a smell almost as striking as the darkness of the place. This smell is strong, physical and earthy, and is redolent of hay, dung and warm milk even though it has been a long time since cows were kept in the shed next to the house. It is a smell that lingers.

Your eye is then drawn to the fire crackling under the black iron cauldron that hangs between two andirons from its chimney hook, and to the sleeping dog by the bench under the mantel of the fireplace, known locally as the *cantou*, almost a room within a

Page 18, and below and opposite: in
the Aveyron in southern France, a
frieze of corn cobs decorates Marcel
and Jean's living room. Near the door
is the small enamel cistern and
basin *(below)* which their parents
used for washing their hands when
they came in from the cowshed. Two
turtle doves are kept for company in a
cage hanging over the door. The old

gun against the wall is a reminder of
autumn shoots. The large hearth or
cantou (right), still contains the armchair made by their father and the
salt-chest, the *banc à sel*. The round
iron stove is still in place, but an
enamelled iron cooker was installed
around 1940, followed by a modern
oven a dozen years ago. A pelmet of
red rep hangs from the mantelpiece.

room. Instinctively you sit down on the bench at the fruitwood table, with the warmth of the fire on your back and in front of you the hunting rifles hanging from the wooden partition which for many years concealed the box-bed.

'I was born in this house in 1920. Just like my father who was born in 1880 and my grandfather who was born I don't remember when,' says Noël who has just come in. He has been out to buy a large round loaf for the week – the price can still be read scrawled in chalk on the crust – and has taken the opportunity to exchange a few words with his neighbours. A delivery van calls daily, stopping at the end of the track leading to the farm. Very talkative and courteous, Noël is still, at the age of seventy-seven, vigorous enough to go out hunting hare with his friends and to play a hand of cards when the old men get together. There is a natural stylishness about his appearance, with a broad beret set well back on his head, trousers hitched up high by a leather belt buckled over his shirt, a woollen pullover and buttoned waistcoat. Over this he wears an open jacket of traditional cotton drill. But he never changes out of his slippers when going down the track to meet the delivery van – 'shoes are for going into town'.

Noël gets out of bed every morning at about seven and his first task is to rekindle the previous night's embers in order to boil water. He then sits down at the table to drink his coffee and to read the paper delivered every morning by his neighbour – a man who still keeps a hundred cows. 'When he's gone that'll be the end of us.

Opposite: this house at Loubaresse in the Massif Central, built a hundred years ago and until 1961 the property of the Allègre family, has been converted into the Ecomuseum of La Margeride. Resisting progress, the Allègre family refused to install electricity and kept the 1950s decor. *Below*: braising dish and glazed earthenware terrine from the region around Nîmes. *Overleaf*: upstairs in the children's bedroom, the bed, a typical *lit à rouleaux* with its scrolled headboard, is covered with a fat feather eiderdown.

At Marcel and Jean's farm, baskets woven from rye straw and bramble are used for storing the round loaves of bread (*opposite, above right*) and the milk cans collected each morning by the milkman (*this page, below*). *Opposite, above left:* this building in the Creuse region serves as an outhouse; *below left:* the Berthalons' house. *This page, top:* a house in the Aveyron region; *centre:* a Savoyard who lives happily with his dog and his cats in an isolated house high in the mountains. *Opposite , below right:* in the Dordogne, the *kibrik,* which is made from willow, is used for washing potatoes in the river. *This page:* double-bottomed basket from the Bourbonnais in central France used for collecting hazelnuts, and above it a basket from the Limousin region, woven from horsechestnut.

One son is an engineer and the other a doctor – people like that aren't going to repopulate this countryside.'

Noël's house was built in the eighteenth century – the date carved into the granite can still be read above the door. In the middle of the Age of Enlightenment, with plague and famine finally eradicated, the first roads were built in the Auvergne. The country people could raise a few pigs and plant potatoes. Noël's house is typical of this period which heralded a new 'civilization'. Absolutely nothing has been altered in the *salle*, which he remembers as his mother's domain and his grandmother's before her. He is upholding their traditions, allowing himself only the smallest alterations. 'This thick oak floor here is good enough for at least another three hundred years....'

Electricity found its way into the house little by little. A light bulb was installed beside the oil lamp, which remained in place just like the candle-holders still standing on the mantelpiece. A water tap has replaced the pump beside the copper cistern, which used to be filled with a pitcher. Noël's parents put in a sink and then fitted an oven in the large fireplace. He has simply carried on where they left off: refrigerator, freezer and gas cooker have taken their place among these innovations, shining cubes lined up by the single window and under that essential piece of domestic decoration – the Post Office calendar. Noël is also the owner of a brand-new television set, but, apart from these modern 'conveniences', everything else is unchanged: the *banc à sel*,

After the Second World War
many country people gave up using
the open fireplace. *Opposite, left
and this page*: the silvered iron stove
of the Berthalons, in the Hautes-
Alpes in the south-east of France,
was bought in 1954 and bears the
maker's signature Le Perreux.
A view of the Drôme, the owner's
birthplace, hangs from the wall as
well as a large photograph of the
grandchildren. Mme Berthalon
made the crocheted blanket herself.
Opposite, right: the brand new
stove in this house in the Beauce in
north-central France is the only
luxury in the living room.

Drôme *provençale*

Left: inside the warm *cantou,* the great hearth, hung with last year's cured hams, this countrywoman in the Cantal in the Auvergne stirs the embers under a pot of potatoes for fattening the pig. It will be killed this winter, between November and February. This ancient and cruel custom can only be carried out with help from the neighbours and the services of a special local slaughterer, or pig-bleeder, who travels from farm to farm and is the only one who knows the secret of a 'clean' kill. Then the year's supply of *charcuterie* – cured hams and sausages – will be made. The wood-fired enamel stove dates from the 1920s.

the bench in which the salt was stored near the fire to keep it dry, tucked into the inglenook, the early nineteenth-century beechwood table with its twin drawers – one for bacon, one for bread – the clock, which 'has never lost a minute', bought at Junhac in 1880, the pinewood dresser made in 1945 in which perishable foodstuffs were kept. As in Noël's mother's time, it is still used for storing pâtés, preserves and liqueurs as well as the old thick-rimmed drinking glasses.

Everything is covered with a fine layer of dust and smuts. It takes some searching to find the earthenware flagon – probably as ancient as the walls themselves – for storing the walnut oil used in salad-dressing and given to the cows 'mixed with *eau de vie* when they have colic'.

In the unheated bedroom Noël piles up baskets, boxes, bottles, umbrellas, apples and coats. His bed, in which both his mother and grandmother gave birth, stands next to the pitchpine cupboard where he keeps his clothes. Like many nineteenth-century country beds, it is a wooden *lit à rouleaux*, a bed with a scrolled headboard. It is virtually submerged beneath several layers of two-coloured, quilted counterpanes – the handiwork of one of the women from the next village who used to make up whatever was required from the cotton or wool that you gave her. On top is a feather eiderdown and beneath are sheets of coarse hemp and linen.

Modern labour-saving appliances do not look at home in this interior architecture with its woodwork, cracked and ancient plaster, old furniture and fireplace. The

Centre: a small portable oven on legs (*potager sur pied*) which holds hot embers and is used for keeping food warm. This one is cast iron with an enamelled top and comes from the Limousin in central France. In other regions the *potager* is often covered with faïence tiles and is an integral part of the furnishings (*see page 72*). *Left*: this rustic pine armchair, made by an old Savoyard, is worthy of Gerrit Rietveld. *Top right*: Noël's house in the Cantal, built of local granite and schist, seems part of the landscape.

furnishings of the house now form an unmatched assortment: they merely coexist in the same way that city dwellers' electronic gadgets sit uneasily with the furnishings of urban apartments. But Noël seems hardly to notice. He is content to go on a while longer, to keep his frail dignity and to carry on the old ways of his parents. For a visitor from town, his house celebrates a physical and sensuous way of living, rooted in memories of the past.

A few kilometres away, Marcel and Jean's farm is pretty much the same. They have set up an armchair and small table just inside the *cantou* where they read and check their accounts. A turtle-dove coos each time one of them goes down the passage leading to the *salle*, which is hung with a thick frieze of maize, a curious memento of a past harvest-home with a neighbour. China bowls and copper saucepans are lovingly displayed on the dresser. The bed is hidden, like the television, in an alcove behind a dark red curtain. Marcel and Jean, who are about ten years younger than Noël, still keep a few animals and are hand-rearing their own pig. Near the dog sleeping on the hearth, potatoes simmer in a huge iron pot. The old wooden table has been exchanged for one topped with Formica, but they still have the old family clock and the blue cistern and basin, decorated with enamel flowers, in which their parents used to wash their hands before sitting down to meals. Living alone on an out-of-the-way hillside

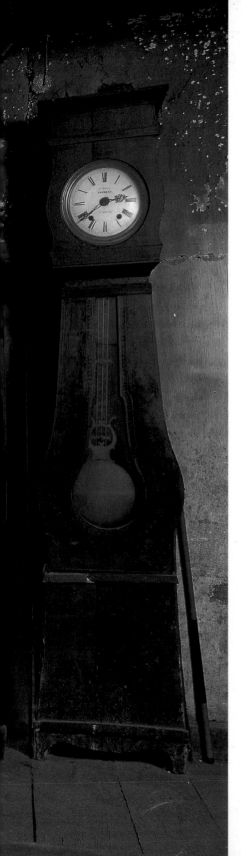

Left: the main room, the
salle, in Noël's house.
He sleeps in the wooden bed,
a *lit à rouleaux (right)* under a
pile of quilts and eiderdowns
worthy of the fairy tale
The Princess and the Pea.

they see very few people. Who can say if they suffer as a result? They never visit the town. They are the sort of men who might one day be found out in the field struck by lightning. Each day sees them pass just a little further along their own solitary way.

In the Hautes-Alpes, the Berthalons' house, opposite a Reformed Church, looks rather like Noël's place from the outside. It is built of schist, timber and earth – local materials taken from the landscape for generations. Built partly underground for warmth, concealed behind a number of narrow openings and with an enormous loft for hay and wood, it is a very rugged-looking building that blends with the landscape – a majestic steep-sided valley overlooking the River Durance. The Berthalons are in their sixties. After sharing the house for many years with their parents, the two of them now live alone. Their children have left to work down in the valley, giving up farming like most of the other villagers.

The uneven walls of the house have been given a coat of beige gloss, while the fireplace and cupboards set into the walls lend the place a very antiquated look, as does the armchair carved by a grandfather back in the 1930s. But the Berthalons have covered the floor with a modern linoleum which matches the oilcloth on the table. Beside the stove is a rustic folding bed made of polished wood with barley-sugar columns and a hand-crocheted coverlet. Mme Berthalon does not do her cooking in the *salle*, but in a small side room opening on to the road, which is also the entrance for visitors. The styles of several generations, the irregular and bumpy walls, the absence of right angles and the lilliputian dimensions of the only window give the place, half-underground, a reassuring, yet bizarre atmosphere. The children will end up by wallpapering the whole place – if they don't sell up first.

Opposite: Noël, who is now seventy-seven years old, often settles down beside his dog on the bench inside the granite-paved *cantou*. The rest of the room has an oak floor dating from the eighteenth century. *Below*: glazed earthenware bowls, or *jattes,* from the Nîmes region.

36

Preceding pages: the beechwood table *(left)* is now lit by electricity, but Noël has kept the oil lamp and soot-blackened candlesticks handed down by his grandparents. His pocket lamps have been hung at the end of the mantelpiece, and near the window *(right)* hangs his Post Office calendar illustrated with shooting and fishing scenes. *Left*: in the dresser, bought by his mother in 1950, Noël stores preserves and jams. The large earthenware jar *(right)*, covered by a flan dish, is used for storing oil and probably dates from the eighteenth century.

EVERYDAY OBJECTS

Pottery and glazed earthenware

France is rich in clays and has a great variety of pottery styles. In the eighteenth century lead glazes came to be widely used; they made containers non-porous, and produced a range of colours through brown, ochre and green. The pottery workshops around Nîmes were famous, notably those at Uzès and Saint-Quentin-la-Poterie. Pottery was used for carrying, cooking, moulding and serving food, as well as for preserving and straining it. Just after the war, new materials and production methods caused a slump. *Above, left to right*: Savoyard water jug of multi-coloured clay; mould from Sarthe for draining freshly made cheese; cooking pot from the Perche for preparing tripe; Savoyard water jug; pot from the Béarn for storing fat. *Centre, left to right*: black-bottomed dish from the Meuse; soup bowl with lugs from the Auvergne; drinking mug *(also shown far right)* from Saint-Quentin-la-Poterie in Provence; heart-shaped cheese strainer from the Perche. *Below, left to right*: Oil jar from the Mâcon region; green water pitcher from the Tarn; twin soup bowl from Normandy for taking food to workers in the fields; Savoyard double mug decorated *à la lune* (with 'moons'); colander from the Auge region.

À LA GROTTE BÉNIE
J'AI PRIÉ POUR VOUS

In the more remote islands off the coast of Brittany – Molène, Sein and Ushant, for example – or in the recesses of deserted valleys in the Alps or the Pyrenees which see the sun for barely eight months of the year, there are still houses to be found whose interiors display values which have almost died out everywhere else: religion – the Saviour and the Sacred Heart, the Virgin Mary and the saints, powers offering protection from the savagery of the elements; the high points of family life – photographs of weddings and first communions, portraits of previous generations and other ghosts of the past. There are trinkets to inspire dreams of voyages to Valparaiso or Tahiti; mementoes of sailors and of those who spent their lives waiting for their return; souvenirs of the bright lights of town, dances, fairs and the Pardons (Breton pilgrimages) – all the gatherings where people met and courted each other.

SYMBOLS

Before the war, all the supplies of the island of Ushant – too wild for fishing and too far from the coast to share in the wealth of the mainland – came by seaborne trade, from those testing voyages from which men returned only after months or even years, if they returned at all. The little houses with their thick stone walls, in which several generations of wives, children and old people lived side by side, were built like ships' cabins, and were decorated like churches. Each corner corresponded to a different room, *le beau bout* (the 'smart' end) serving as the sitting room and *le vilain bout* (the 'ugly' end) doing duty as the kitchen. Moving from one to the other involved squeezing through a passage every bit as narrow as a ship's gangway and picking one's way through a mass of bric-à-brac, a maze of cupboard-clocks, coffer-benches, tables-cum-bread-troughs, chimney cupboards and enclosed box-beds. All the houses on

the island followed the same plan, which dictated the course of day-to-day existence by assigning to everyone a particular task and place within the family hierarchy.

As there were no trees, timber was obtained from the sea. The salvaged debris of wrecked ships and assorted flotsam was collected, and then brightly decorated with whatever remained of the paint used on the small boats taken out in the summer, weather permitting. Poverty was concealed under bright colours – blue (symbolic of the Virgin Mary), bright green, brown (smart and discreet), red, and so on: there were schemes of two or even three colours, a charming feature of these wooden interiors, which elsewhere in Brittany are generally very gloomy.

Above fireplaces, on dressers, on the walls or hanging from roofbeams, there are ships in bottles or cut-away models of boats, oilskins and mariners' kitbags painted with nautical motifs (brought back as souvenirs of distant voyages by husbands, fathers and sons), all jostling with pink seashells from Bora Bora and blue butterflies from Brazil. Images of the Virgin of Marseilles, the port where sailors first came ashore, take their place beside Chinese Buddhas and mermaids from the brothels of Hong Kong. Multicoloured glass globes decorate austere crucifixes and the little wreaths of artificial flowers kept in memory of departed children.

Nowadays there are very few of these old-style houses to be found on the island, although it is buffeted by winds and storms that are as fierce as ever. We are deeply touched by their naive poetry wherever we happen to come upon them, even if only in a museum, even if we feel that they reflect narrow and unchanging values.

Alsace is a region as devout as Brittany – particularly in the Bas-Rhin. Here the houses display crucifixes and other religious icons, and a wealth of unsophisticated scenes, painted on glass, of the Virgin Mary or stories from the Bible. These naive images of devotion form a noticeable contrast to the austere interiors typical of

Page 44: Dresser from
Ushant, Brittany.

Pages 46–47: Augustine's garden,
facing the majestic Massif du
Pelvoux in the Hautes-Alpes, looks
like a modern art installation with
its strange mixture of utilitarian
objects, vivid colours and a
profusion of flowers.

This page and overleaf: Augustine's
kitchen with its multi-coloured floor
covering and tablecloth, old door
and modern coffee pot.

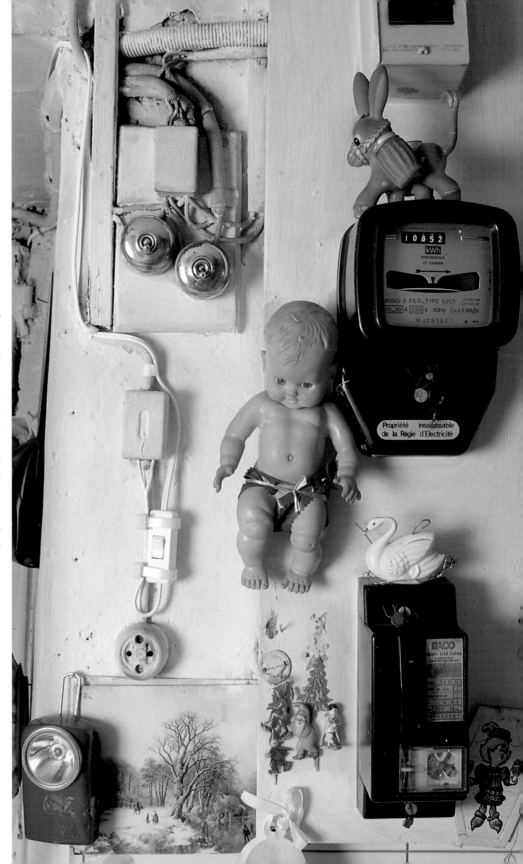

In Augustine's house the theatrical nylon curtains, plastic vine leaves and bouquets of flowers *(opposite)*, greeting card, little Santa Clauses for decorating cakes, dwarfs, the rubber swan and the baby doll *(right)* bring back happy memories to compensate for the material hardships and lack of comfort. The bright colours and man-made materials bring a breath of the town to this old house high up in the Hautes-Alpes, investing it with the cheerful charm once found in the concierge's lodge or the gypsy caravan.

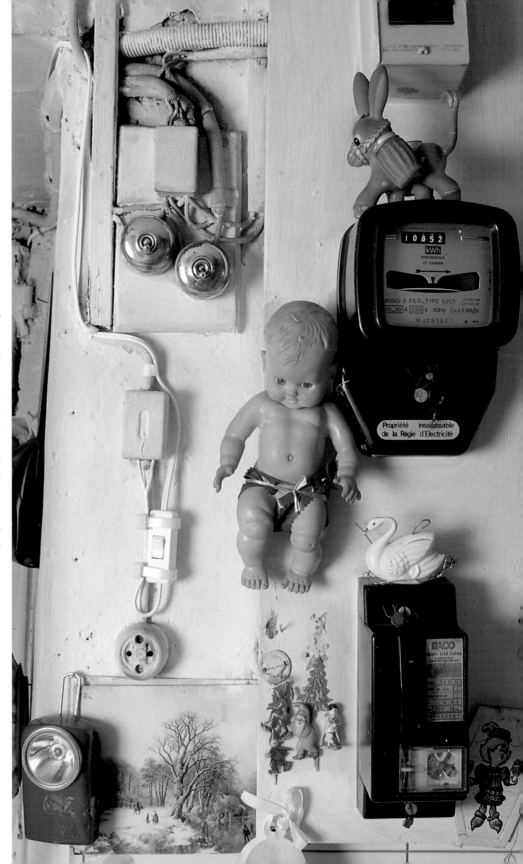

52

areas that are less devoutly Catholic, such as the Auvergne in south-central France, the Nord in the north east or the Hautes-Alpes where Augustine's house is.

Somewhere between Nice and Grenoble, not far from the Italian border and perched above a village clinging to the mountainside, is Augustine's house. With its profusion of snowy plastic lace curtains, artificial flowers and various souvenirs, this home is completely different from its neighbours, and makes us feel as if we were in another world. Many steep steps lead to the little gate that opens into the garden where geraniums, cyclamen, begonias, gladioli and phlox bloom under the obviously green fingers of their owner. Although eighty-six, she radiates a zest for life. 'It rained every day this summer,' she remarks with philosophical resignation. She now lives alone

and, from November to March, has to clear the snow herself from the steps, the garden and the pathway to reach the delivery van where she buys her provisions. Her family once owned cows and fields, but she still had to go and find work in Grenoble during the winter months to make ends meet. It was an opportunity to explore another world – the town. It was a chance to meet people with values and ways of life different from those of her own family, and to experience new places and new pleasures – fairs, festivals and shops. Today Augustine lives in three rooms: a kitchen and two bedrooms, one of which serves as her sitting room. From the kitchen door there is an unobstructed view over the impressive Massif du Pelvoux, if you can only tear your eyes away from the unbelievable amount of clutter blocking the entrance, the chaotic disorder which forms a barrier between the outside world and her own domain. On closer inspection the confusion of piled-up boxes, tights hanging up to dry, bits of wood, bowls, potted

Left: this sailor from Finistère is wearing the traditional seaman's cap, leather boots and thick socks known as *beguen*. The inside of his house is like a web woven by time, reflecting the influence of the sea, religious traditions and family

history (*above*)– like the early nineteenth-century dresser from Ushant in Brittany (*overleaf*) which displays an effigy of the Virgin Mary from Marseilles surrounded by Sarreguemines crockery and porcelain from China.

Like the cemetery on the Breton island of Molène *(above left)*, the houses on Ushant are gaudily decorated inside – almost kitsch. *Below*: Virgin of Saint-Malo under a glass dome. *Opposite, right*: a ship in a bottle, a picture of the Sacred Heart

that was bought from a pedlar and Chinese porcelain brought back from distant sea voyages. *Below left*: another picture of the Sacred Heart behind a stack of Japanese porcelain cups and saucers.

plants and other unlikely articles has in fact a very definite structure and logic. In its way, it reflects the world of this elderly woman and her struggle against isolation. Like the garden, the inside of Augustine's home is brightly cheerful. There are many-coloured plastic flowers, stuffed toy animals, picture postcards and pictures in gilded frames. There are plastic dolls, pieces of wrapping paper and empty bottles. All this is displayed against a background of oilcloths, Formica, lace, linoleum and wallpaper, as well as unmatched pieces of flower-patterned carpet. This deliberate style – rather kitsch – is reminiscent of a gypsy caravan or an old-fashioned concierge's lodge. But all the little presents and souvenirs – barometers, miniature chalets and assorted bunches of flowers, mementoes of outings to fairs (perhaps the fair at Briançon

only half an hour away by car) – are really reminders of affection, serving to shut out the harshness of a hardworking life, to keep loneliness at bay. There is so much love invested in Augustine's home.

A traditional granite cottage on Ushant *(left)*, with its simple, almost severe façade built to withstand the violence of Atlantic storms. Inside *(opposite)*, driftwood has been used from floor to ceiling to build an interior like a ship's cabin.

As for the extravagant and elaborate floor coverings in the bedroom and kitchen, she saw them one day at a friend's – 'a cowherd on the Col du Galibier' – who obligingly gave her the address of the shop where her nephews could buy them for her. Is this so different from the fashion codes, snobberies and influences of the modern city, whether it is Paris, London or New York?

Isolation, lack of means and exclusion from the consumer society leads to a craving for compensation from the world of the imagination. On the island of Ushant in Brittany, it is this that creates a theatrical setting for the fixed routines of everyday existence. In other places, equally remote and isolated, deprivation can sometimes stimulate a wild and unbridled creativity.

Left: on the island of Ushant, above the traditional fireplace, enclosed to protect it from draughts, stand a Chinese Buddha and pots decorated with Millet's famous *Angelus* – one of the most popular works of art with country people.

Gloss painted every year at Easter – in blue, the Virgin Mary's own colour – this old seafarer's house still has its traditional table with the drawer for storing bread *(above)*, which exactly fits into the canted window recess.

Right and below: the Ecomuseum at Niou on the island of Ushant. In the houses on this island each mantelpiece is a record of

the family history, its travels, its piety and its dreams, as well as giving a clear indication of its social standing.

EVERYDAY OBJECTS

Stoneware, faïence and porcelain

Until the 1950s it was the custom for Breton sailors, leaving ship at Marseilles or Le Havre, to bring back souvenirs of their voyages to distant lands – statues of Buddha from China and Japan, fish-shaped vases, precious and ornately decorated porcelain services. Now that such things are seen everywhere, it is difficult to imagine their almost magical power when they were first brought back to the sailors' cottages, with exotic shells, flower-bulbs and occasionally a talking parrot. *Lower right*: very common in France, this heat-resistant kitchenware, sometimes known as *terre de fer* (ironstone), was produced during the nineteenth century at Saint-Uze and Saint-Vallier in the Drôme. The blue-and-white check patterned jug *(opposite, right)* was made at Sarreguemines, as were most of the bowls, if not at Digoin or Saint-Amand. The famous blue-and-grey stoneware of Betschdorf in Alsace *(opposite, below right)*, made from the alum-rich local clay and decorated with cobalt blue, was already being made in the seventeenth century. Young brides' garlands of orange blossom were displayed, like the effigies of the Virgin Mary, under glass domes or in glittering caskets, with gilded wreaths, glass trinkets and family photographs.

Marie Laharie's house in the Landes, just like Juliette Mathurin's in the Hautes-Alpes, is calm, empty, meticulously clean – the architecture and the light dominate. Both houses reflect a tradition as yet untouched by the consumer society and the cult of excess: here everything has a function. Such a minimalist way of life might be the very thing to tempt the taste of our own time, tired by shallow fripperies, except that this austerity is dictated by extreme poverty and, at times, by an isolation which makes contact with the outside world almost impossible. Until the 1950s, these houses were still full of life, and fulfilled the needs of a family group and the surrounding village life. Nowadays they seem cold and comfortless.

Old Marie Laharie looks just like Little Red Riding Hood's grandmother – like some benevolent sorceress, one of those magic beings, primitive and ageless, encountered

BARE ESSENTIALS

in the depths of the forest. She makes claim, in fact, to modest healing powers and is well versed in herb lore. Quite small, round as a pumpkin, with grey hair twisted into a bun, roughened plump little hands behind her back and her ample stomach covered by an apron of homespun black satinette, Marie is a sturdy woman whose character has been tried and tested throughout a lifetime of extreme poverty.

To reach her house it is necessary first of all to turn off the road which runs straight through the immense coastal pine forest of the Landes, and to take the winding, sandy track – recently tarred over – leading to the hamlet where she lives: her *quartier*, as the local people say, which is a handful of cottages huddled together in a clearing surrounded by oak trees, known as an *airial*. It is a marshy area. If you set off across some small rivulet trickling through the heather, half hidden by the long grass,

Page 68: Marie Laharie's house, living-room window. *Right*: door leading from the living room to the bedroom with its old mirrored armoire. In the *salle (left and overleaf)* the mantelpiece displays Marie's father's old candlesticks, and also her mother's paraffin lamp, kept well polished, one of the few slightly frivolous luxuries in this room, together with the artificial lace, vase of fresh flowers and the green pelmet (bought in 1983) above the hearth.

Right: standing among her potatoes, narcissi, leeks, irises and lettuce, Marie often watches the deer pass by on the edge of the forest while she waters her garden. Her house *(opposite, above right)* is deep in a great wild forest, like a forest from a fairy tale. *Opposite below*: metal cheese-strainer. *Overleaf*: Marie's austere bedroom.

you invariably come across one of those curious huts made of fern which are used as shooting hides by hunters of the *palombe*, the wild wood pigeon of the region. One suddenly realizes just how

remote this place is. In the depths of the forest the silence, broken only by the sounds of fluttering and of rustling grass, is quite extraordinary. Marie Laharie is seventy-nine and does not drive. She has used her pension to buy a car for her niece whose twice-weekly visits keep her stocked with provisions. Apart from her niece, she sees no one else except occasionally the postman. She has green fingers and still tends her vegetable patch, partly given over to growing flowers, and she keeps a few hens. She has a taste for life. She has worked since she was fourteen, and as 'maid of all work' or daily help to 'other folk', and so has known harder times. She only cares about the death of Jules her tenant-farmer husband, six years ago.

Marie's house is utterly typical – you can see one very similar in the Ecomuseum at Maquèze. Its roof, made of the local pink, sharply curved tiles, reaches down quite low, giving the structure that graceful shape resembling a dove's tail. It was built in the nineteenth century when the use of pine became widespread, and the commercial exploitation of turpentine – a derivative of resin – began to replace sheep-farming as the staple of the region's economy. Marie's house turns its back to the west wind which blows from the sea, and looks instead towards the sunrise. Its walls are made of oak, with a mixture of straw and mud filling the spaces between the vertical posts and cross-timbers.

This harmonious building was built straight on to the grass in the field. It has no porch and the front door opens directly into the living room from under the vine that here, as elsewhere in the region, girdles the entire house and its outbuildings – hen-house, hayloft, pigsty and woodshed. Only fifty years ago, the buildings formed part of a structured community, or *quartier*, with its own hierarchy and proper allocation of labour, its annual cycle of festivals and rituals.

Marie Laharie remembers those days even though she now has only her dog for company. She came to settle in the *airial* in 1933 when she married – 'to be where the work was'. All the internal fittings of the house date from that time. Marie does not recall having bought anything since, except the green

cloth for the mantelshelf (in 1983) – 'I wash it in vinegar to keep the colour because I like it' – and a cooker and a refrigerator. These are both installed in the scullery at the back of the house where there is also a sink which Marie uses for both her personal toilette and the washing-up. The living room and bedroom display all the austerity of a minimalist loft, which accentuates the timber-framed structure of the building, the fireplace and the low ceiling. The walls are completely covered with a lemon-yellow wash, the skirting and woodwork are painted a blue-grey. The red tiling of the floor has become somewhat uneven.

Marie's exuberant geraniums have almost completely obscured the windows. There is always a vase of fresh flowers on the table with its machine-made lace cloth. The place is neat, strangely empty, with a certain luminosity and serenity. It appeals to us because this way of living is disappearing. The bed which stands in this room was a

Left and opposite: Juliette's house, in the Hautes-Alpes. 'My poor husband left me enough firewood to last me the rest of my life when he went to join our Lord,' she says sighing. Keeping warm is essential in the hostile climate of these mountains. Fitted kitchens are unknown here, and the gas cooker *(left)* is rather at odds with a room whose style has not been altered since 1940, and whose charm lies in the simplicity of its architecture, its coloured walls and its emptiness.

A medieval farmhouse in the Haute-Savoie, whose walls are being eaten away by saltpetre. A neon strip-light is attached directly on to the ceiling and the telephone is fixed to the wall, like the electricity meter hidden behind the cotton floral-patterned curtain. The Formica-topped table and ceramic 'sandstone' floor date from the 1950s, and are the most modern features to be found in the entire house.

wedding present from Marie's parents – they also gave the sheets, blankets and mattress. Marie and her husband ordered everything else from a joiner in Sabres, the neighbouring small town – the armoire, washstand (with water jug and basin of Sarreguemines china), the mirror and pine bedside table. She treasures a crucifix made of mahogany which she was given on the day of her first communion. As for the chairs, they once belonged to her mother who was given them as a wedding present. Marie has arranged them rather curiously against the wall as if in prepara-

tion for her own funerary vigil.

In the living room, whose furniture was also ordered from Sabres at the same time, there is an open fireplace with embers always glowing on the hearth. 'People call my house an ice-box,' says Marie, 'but the fire is all the heating I've got.' She often sits close to the fire, brooding over the past. On the mantelshelf is an artillery shell from the 1914–18 war, brought back by her grandfather, as well as her father's little brass candlesticks. Next to them stands the most ancient object in the house, reputed to be over a hundred years old: a clock bought in Sabres by her grandfather. Every item conjures up a piece of Marie's family history, nothing is simply there for decoration.

Marie Laharie loves to be surrounded by all the things which remind her of the past and which bring both joy and despair. She has known many griefs. She has worked like a beast of burden, and talks and mutters all the time, launching into incoherent long monologues. Completely deaf, her life is now confined to a world of plants, streams, birds and animals. Her heart beats to the rhythm of the forest that surrounds her house and which she knows will keep her alive for the time that she has left.

Some of the most attractive rural cottages are found in the south west of France. *Opposite, above*: a cottage in the Aveyron; *below*: a farm in the forest of the Landes. The Musée des Landes at Marquèze, south of Bordeaux, is, with Ushant's museum, one of the earliest and finest of the French Ecomuseums, set up under the influence of Georges Rivière in the 1970s. Deep in the forest, the buildings of an entire hamlet have been rebuilt to show how such communities were organized, both indoors and out. *Left*: the veranda of one of the houses belonging to the hamlet.

During the nineteenth century, farmers of means attached great importance to their daughters' trousseau preparations. The bride was expected to provide the household linen for her new home,

and it was made from flax and hemp grown and harvested on the family farm. It was woven on narrow looms which explains why there are seams running down the middle. The linen was generally embroidered with initials in cross stitch.

Mattresses and counterpanes

In the Ecomuseum at Marquèze this bed (*left*), with valance hooked directly on to the rafters, takes up practically the whole room. Made in the Landes in 1889, it imitates the bourgeois taste of the previous century. In a marriage contract of the time it was stipulated that a young bride of the Landes should provide a trousseau consisting of the following: counterpanes, valances, headboards and bed curtains of linen and quilted cotton check, cotton 'ceiler' or canopy, feather bed and pillows in twill, mattress ticking, and several different kinds of sheets: for example, one of linen, four of hemp, two of fine linen, four of hemp and flax mixture. The bride also had to bring napkins, tablecloths and kitchen cloths. When the name of her future husband was known she would embroider his initials, in cross stitch, opposite her own. The contents of a trousseau varied according to means.

Right: twill, mattress ticking and *kelsh*. Made in Alsace from flax, sometimes mixed with cotton or hemp, *kelsh* is the fabric used to cover pillows and eiderdowns as well as mattresses. Rather like Scottish tartans, patterns and colours identified their owners and the families they came from.

EVERYDAY OBJECTS

Counterpanes

In the nineteenth century, curtained beds – the four-poster and the *lit d'ange* with drapes from a canopy attached to the wall – gradually gave way to beds known as *lits bateaux* with headboard and footboard or *lits à rouleaux* with scrolled ends (*see pages 25 and 35*). Equipped with one, two or even three mattresses stuffed with straw, horsehair, seaweed, feathers or chaff (for children's beds) – and perhaps a feather bolster or pillows – they were covered with multicoloured layers of quilted counterpanes over which was thrown a thick feather eiderdown, usually red. In the Massif Central, where it can be very cold, quilted coverlets were thick and soft, unlike the thin, light *boutis* of Provence. Uncarded wool was sandwiched between two layers of contrasting printed cotton fabric bought in town or from a travelling pedlar, and made up by a local needlewoman.

The period immediately after the Second World War saw great changes in the domestic interiors of country working people. Couples who were married between 1940 and 1950, now in their seventies, live in houses decorated and furnished in a style quite different from those who married before the war. From the start they had the benefit of all 'mod cons', and they have never been without electricity. While recognizing the benefits of progress in planning their living space, they have taken care to keep some traditional elements. Their main consideration has been to make their homes bright, clean, well-lit and easy to look after; they remember rooms in their parents' time as gloomy, smoky, comfortless and unwelcoming. In these 'transitional' houses there is usually both a kitchen and a sitting room, and one or more bedrooms besides. There is no flush lavatory, but electricity meters and boilers

HYBRID STYLE

are commonplace. Refrigerators, washing-machines and cookers – generally white, or brown and beige – are conspicuously on show, rather as the 2CV or Panhard was parked ostentatiously outside the front door in the 1950s.

Seen from outside, the windows are a continuation of the internal decor, a kind of 'window dressing' which has to be spruce and neat. They generally overflow with flowers – begonias, geraniums and sage – predominantly red. Since the 1980s they have boasted a new decorative element: the nylon *trompe l'œil* curtain which presents idyllic country scenes and other classic images of bliss: a cat under the moon, a setting sun behind palm trees, a seventeenth-century frigate under full sail, or some creature in a sunbonnet sipping through a straw. 'Made to measure, ready to fit', these popular icons are the latest refinements of the 'plastic tablecloth style'.

Since 1980 there has been a move from red-and-white or blue-and-white gingham in favour of the more discreet ivory, beige or brown, which suits any part of the house from the kitchen to the *salle*. Bouquets and baskets of flowers, grasses and bull-rushes, birds, bunches of grapes or garlands of leaves entwined with stripes and tartan patterns decorate the oilcloths on the tables, and are more or less co-ordinated with the wallpaper, or 'wall covering' as it is now called whether vinyl or not. These wallpapers are frequently changed – once every two years seems to be the ideal.

There is also a preference for shades of brown for the floor, the speckled and glazed stoneware tiles of the 1940s having given way to mass-produced glazed so-called *tomettes*. Those with more modest budgets generally favour a lightly embossed linoleum imitating wooden parquet: it reflects the neon strip-lighting from the ceiling above.

Against this modern backdrop, characteristic items of furniture and family heirlooms constitute the main difference between these 'transitional' rural interiors and those of the urban working classes. The architecture, first of all, is unchanged with its open beams – often deliberately preserved – thick walls, double-casement windows and old-fashioned fireplaces inside which a stove is now preferred even where the original mantelpiece survives. Certain details of the old style have been kept: the brass ornaments; the china pots and the tins for storing sugar, salt and flour; the ancient alarm-clock; the crucifix; the candlesticks; the copper pots and pans; and the long-case clock which nearly always stands opposite the front door. The long-case clock first appeared in farmhouses at the end of the eighteenth century but became a common feature during the nineteenth; it is always the last piece to leave the house for the secondhand dealer. At Morez in the Franche-Comté, 3000 were

Page 90: in Mme Neuvic's kitchen, in the Auvergne in south-central France, a wood-fired stove and gas oven now occupy the old hearth brightly decked out with gold-trimmed pelmet. An embossed imitation parquet linoleum covers the floor, and the walls have been papered. *Opposite*: the bedroom belonging to M. and Mme Blondeau, in the Perche region in northern France. The armoire dates from the nineteenth century, the satin eiderdown on the bed is a reminder of the past, but the central light, like the bed, was bought in the 1950s.

92

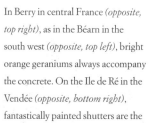

In Berry in central France *(opposite, top right)*, as in the Béarn in the south west *(opposite, top left)*, bright orange geraniums always accompany the concrete. On the Ile de Ré in the Vendée *(opposite, bottom right)*, fantastically painted shutters are the

talk of the neighbours, while on the island of Molène, Brittany, *(left)* a use is found for unfinished pots of paint left over from refurbishing the boats. In the gardens of Ushant, Brittany, *(opposite, far left)* are miniature reproductions of the island's old windmills.

95

made in 1830, and 36,000 in 1846. They were made of painted wood, and were dismantled before being transported by rail and then reassembled in place or in the workshop of a clockmaker in the nearest town.

As for the sideboard and the dresser full of china, these are put either in the kitchen or in the *salle*. Often over a century old, the sideboard is well suited to the stiff and inhospitable *salle*. This cold room is rarely used apart from family gatherings, baptisms, weddings and funerals, and perhaps for sewing and ironing, for these days the 'sitting rooms' of country farmhouses ape those of the bourgeoisie. This is where the

valuable glass and china are carefully kept, with the photos of men in military uniform, brides and first communicants, and also the carved and painted stags and Alsatian dogs, dolls with elaborate hairstyles and sequinned dresses – for the most part soulless, mass-produced objects of obscure pedigree. On the table, in the very centre of a doily and below a 1960s ceiling lamp of frosted glass, a Louis-the-something-style china soup tureen sits in state – never to be used, of course. This is the room where the aquarium usually goes, and where tender

plants, such as begonias or azaleas, are brought in from the cold. The television set, by contrast, is kept in the kitchen, often on top of the fridge. There too, is the old wireless with rounded lines and gilt trimmings. It no longer works , but it is displayed on top of a small set of shelves trimmed with a frill.

Bedrooms, the only places of privacy, follow the same pattern almost everywhere in rural areas: double bed, night tables (with chamber pot or sanitary bucket), armoire with or without looking-glass, chairs and dressing-table – preferably pine – ordered for the newly-weds from a local joiner. Sometimes, however, the armoire is an old

In the Perche in northern France, M. Blondeau has hung above his nineteenth-century sideboard a photograph of the château where he worked as a gardener all his life, and where he received the Medal of Merit from the local agricultural society. His grandmother's bridal crown, protected by a glass dome, stands next to photographs of his children and grandchildren. On the opposite side of the room, artillery shells brought back by his father from the 1914–18 war are lined up above the fireplace with a lamp dating from pre-electric days *(opposite)*. A brown and beige wallpaper is the backdrop for these souvenirs.

Left and below: in this kitchen
in northern France, belonging to
M. and Mme Bureau, coffee
is always ready in the aluminium

pot. In this beige and brown room
all the furniture is new. Only a
cupboard and a few chairs have
survived from the past.

piece and was a grandparent's wedding present; in Normandy these are often carved with entwined doves. Old too are the family portraits from the early 1900s, the feather eiderdown, the crucifix or the rosary.

In the Pas-de-Calais the domestic interiors of the Demarescaux and Bureau families are typical of these 'transitional' decors, now to be seen throughout France. Born in the early 1920s, the two couples were married just after the war. Both families were given the furniture for bedroom and *salle* as wedding presents, and they have inherited pieces from the last two generations. Their farmhouses both date from the mid-nineteenth century when bricks and tiles began to be mass-produced. At that time a whole region stretching from northern Flanders to Picardy was dotted with these huge, austere square buildings which can still be seen today – brick-red or whitewashed, with enormous foundation bases painted black or grey – enclosing a central courtyard. One couple makes cider, the other breeds the traditional heavy horses of the Nord, this region of France. Neither has a bathroom or an inside lavatory. It is this lack of modern plumbing that forms the greatest contrast between the generations, for young couples still keep up the old ways of their parents in their cold and formal sitting rooms contrasting with cosy kitchens for everyday living. In the kitchen coffee is always ready on the gently purring stove, and the table is always welcoming. Although all appears a bit too clean, scoured and functional, the all-purpose kitchen in this part of France reflects a true sense of the art of domestic living. Rather like the old houses of the Auvergne, they are civilized. Coffee will be served in yellow transparent Pyrex or Duralex tumblers, in white Arcopal decorated with transfers of flowers or fruit, or occasionally in a thick china bowl. If there is something lacking in these materialistic yet pleasing homes, it is that they no longer have a strong identity – an authentic regional flavour.

Large exotic flowers cover the wallpaper in M. and Mme Bureau's bedroom. They were given the furniture as a wedding present in 1944. The novelty frame holding a photograph of their granddaughter in her first communion dress dates from 1970.

Overleaf: their dining-room – rather formal with its artificial lace and flowery wallpaper – is used only on special occasions such as betrothals, baptisms and funerals.

Opposite, below: leisure time in the Demarescaux kitchen in the Pas-de-Calais. They still breed the old heavy horses. They have kept the faïence tiles on the walls and above the sink *(right)*.

Opposite, above: in this kitchen in the Béarn, in central France, the ancient clock from Franche-Comté and the tall dresser have been piously preserved. *Above*: enamelled iron coffee pots.

Left: the bedroom furniture of the Demarescaux was a wedding present. The eiderdown dates from their parents' time.

The two portraits *(above)* come from a peasant cottage in the Creuse in central France, and date from the beginning of this century.

Synthetic materials are easy to keep clean and to change, and these man-made fabrics (*left and right*), nearly all from the Far East, have invaded the French country way of life.

EVERYDAY OBJECTS

Kitchen utensils

The enamel coffee pot *(opposite)* is a symbol of country hospitality. *This page*: kitchen utensils – milk cans *(bottom left)*, colanders *(bottom right)*, saucepans, ladles and skimmers, containers for matches *(top right)*, for salt, flour or rice – show a wide range of decorative styles and come in many shapes and sizes. Brown speckled with grey, or all white, they are either left plain or patterned with squares or spots. Coffee pots with their simple classic form were often covered with exuberant patterns. At the turn of the century, enamel gradually began to make way for aluminium which is more heat resistant. As for the famous stock cubes known as *bouillon Kub* invented by the Maggi company in 1890 *(centre left)*, they are sadly no longer sold in the charming tin boxes which were once so useful for storing corks, keys and bits of string. The coffee grinders *(top left)*, were clasped between the thighs to hold them steady while the handle was turned. They were in common use at the beginning of the century, but now they are a thing of the past.

Allumettes

BOUILLON KUB

GUIDE

Most of the interiors illustrated in this book are
private homes. This Guide gives a selection of the many
museums showing regional French art and crafts
and reconstructions of traditional houses.
It also lists some of the countless shops specializing
in French country furniture, objects and textiles.

Page 112: basket made of chestnut from the Creuse
(central France), with faïence dishes and enamelware.

BRITTANY

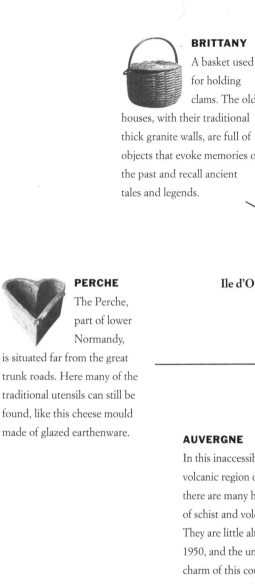

A basket used for holding clams. The old houses, with their traditional thick granite walls, are full of objects that evoke memories of the past and recall ancient tales and legends.

PERCHE

The Perche, part of lower Normandy, is situated far from the great trunk roads. Here many of the traditional utensils can still be found, like this cheese mould made of glazed earthenware.

AUVERGNE

In this inaccessible and volcanic region of France there are many houses made of schist and volcanic stone. They are little altered since 1950, and the undeniable charm of this countryside remains unspoilt.

LANDES

Bridal soup tureen. In the Landes there are still delightful hamlets, little groups of houses made of the local clay. Hidden in the *airials,* or clearings, deep in the woods, they can be difficult to find.

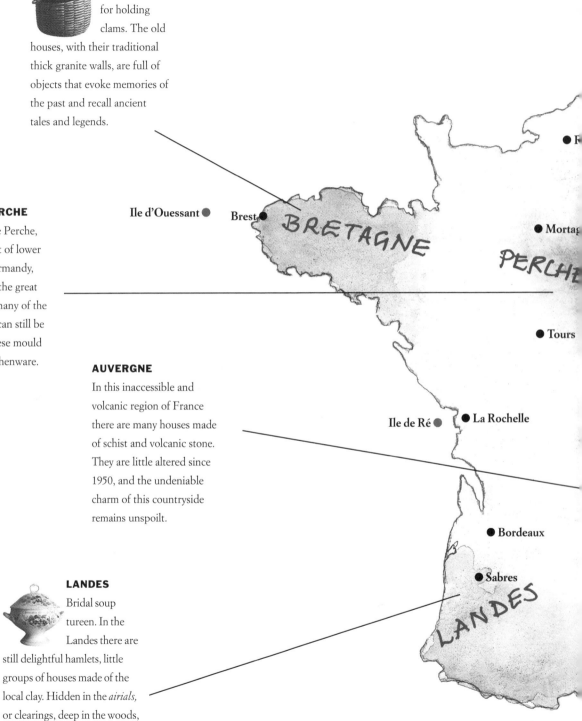

Ile d'Ouessant ●   Brest ●

BRETAGNE

● R

● Mortag

PERCHE

● Tours

Ile de Ré ●   ● La Rochelle

● Bordeaux

● Sabres

LANDES

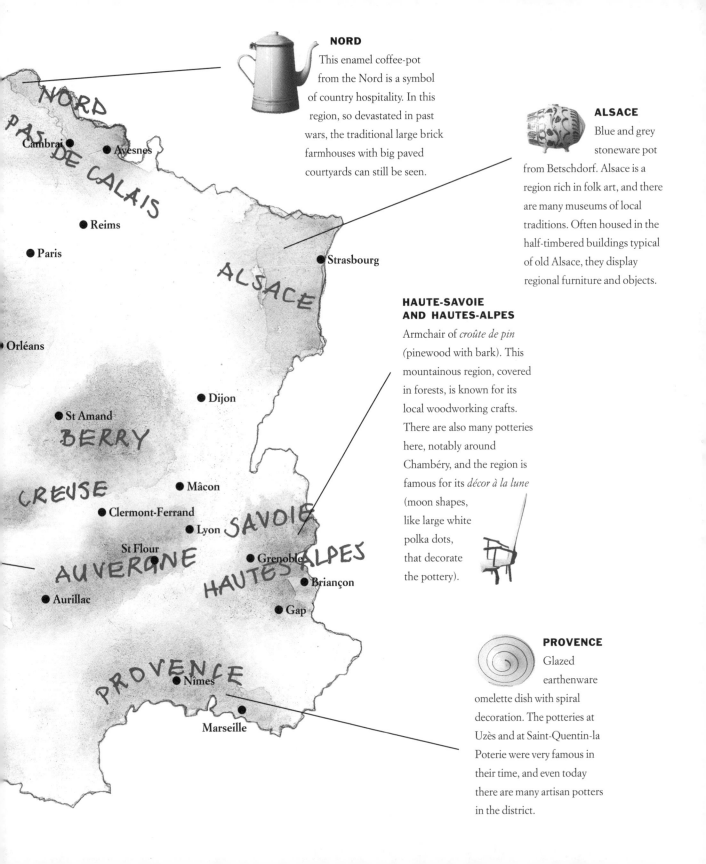

NORD

This enamel coffee-pot from the Nord is a symbol of country hospitality. In this region, so devastated in past wars, the traditional large brick farmhouses with big paved courtyards can still be seen.

ALSACE

Blue and grey stoneware pot from Betschdorf. Alsace is a region rich in folk art, and there are many museums of local traditions. Often housed in the half-timbered buildings typical of old Alsace, they display regional furniture and objects.

HAUTE-SAVOIE AND HAUTES-ALPES

Armchair of *croûte de pin* (pinewood with bark). This mountainous region, covered in forests, is known for its local woodworking crafts. There are also many potteries here, notably around Chambéry, and the region is famous for its *décor à la lune* (moon shapes, like large white polka dots, that decorate the pottery).

PROVENCE

Glazed earthenware omelette dish with spiral decoration. The potteries at Uzès and at Saint-Quentin-la Poterie were very famous in their time, and even today there are many artisan potters in the district.

NORD
PAS DE CALAIS
Cambrai
Avesnes
Reims
Paris
ALSACE
Orléans
Strasbourg
Dijon
St Amand
BERRY
CREUSE
Mâcon
Clermont-Ferrand
Lyon
SAVOIE
St Flour
AUVERGNE
Grenoble
HAUTES-ALPES
Aurillac
Briançon
Gap
PROVENCE
Nîmes
Marseille

MUSEUMS

PARIS

MUSÉE DES ARTS ET TRADITIONS POPULAIRES
6 rue Mahatma Gandhi, 75016 Paris.
Tel: 01 44 17 60 00

CENTRAL FRANCE

ECOMUSÉE DE MARGERIDE
ET HAUTE-AUVERGNE
15320 Ruynes en Margeride.
Tel: 04 71 23 42 96

MUSÉE DES ARTS ET TRADITIONS
POPULAIRES DU PERCHE
Prieuré, Sainte-Gauburge, 61130
Saint-Cyr-la-Rosière. Tel: 02 33 73 48 06

MUSÉE RÉGIONAL D'AUVERGNE
10 bis rue Delille, 63200 Riom.
Tel: 04 73 38 17 31

WESTERN FRANCE

ECOMUSÉE DES MONTS D'ARRÉE
Moulin de Kerhouat, 29450 Commana.
Tel: 02 98 68 87 76

ECOMUSÉE DU NIOU
29242 Ouessant. Tel: 02 98 48 86 37

ECOMUSÉE DE SAINT-DEGAN
Saint-Degan, 56400 Brech.
Tel: 02 97 57 66 00

MAISON DU LIN
27350 Routot. Tel: 02 32 56 21 76

MAISON DE LA MARIÉE
130 île de Fédrun,
44720 Saint-
Joachim.
Tel: 02 40 88
42 04

PROVENCE

MUSÉE DU
VIEUX NÎMES
Place aux Herbes,
30000 Nîmes.
Tel: 04 66 36 00 64

MUSÉE CHARLES DEMERY
39 rue Proudhon, 13150 Tarascon.
Tel: 04 90 91 08 80

MUSÉON ARLATAN
29 rue de la République, 13200 Arles.
Tel: 04 90 93 58 11

SOUTH WEST FRANCE

ECOMUSÉE DE LA GRANDE LANDE
Marquèze, 40630 Sabres.
Tel: 05 58 07 52 70

MUSÉE CASA PAIRAL
Le Castillet, place de Verdun,
66000 Perpignan. Tel: 04 68 35 42 05

MUSÉE CÉVENNOL
Rue Calquières, 30120 Le Vigan.
Tel: 04 67 81 06 86

EASTERN FRANCE

ECOMUSÉE D'ALSACE
Grosswald, 68190 Ungersheim.
Tel: 03 89 74 44 44

LA FERME DE MONTAGNON
La Maison Myotte Noël, Hameau
de Grandfontaine, 25390 Orchamps-Vennes.
Tel: 03 81 43 57 86

MUSÉE ALSACIEN
23 quai Saint-Nicolas, 67000 Strasbourg.
Tel: 03 88 35 55 36
One of the finest folk art museums in France,
installed in a 17th-century house typical
of the region.

MUSÉE DE L'IMAGERIE PEINTE
ET POPULAIRE ALSACIENNE
38 rue du Dr Albert Schweitzer,
67350 Pfaffenhoffen.
Tel: 03 88 72 26 60

MUSÉE DE LA POTERIE
2 rue Kuhlendorf, 67660 Betschdorf.
Tel: 03 88 54 48 07

This list is a selection from more than 400 museums
in France showing collections of local
and traditional material. Many are open to the
public only from April to October.

For further information contact: FÉDÉRATION
DES ECOMUSÉES ET MUSÉES DE SOCIÉTÉ,
4 square Castan, 25031 Besançon.
Tel: 03 81 83 22 55

SOURCES

FRANCE

PARIS

ARLETTE TIXIER
41 quai de l'Horloge, 75001 Paris.
Tel: 01 43 54 21 43
Furniture and antiques, folk art

CUISINOPHILIE
28 rue du Bourg-Tibourg, 75004 Paris.
Tel: 01 40 29 07 32
Enamel and tinware, 1950s kitchenware,
china and glazed earthenware

FANETTE
1 rue d'Alençon, 75015 Paris.
Tel: 01 42 22 21 73
China, furniture, household linen and quilts

HUGUETTE BERTRAND
22 rue Jacob, 75006 Paris. Tel: 01 43 26 59 08
Furniture and antiques

SAINT-OUEN FLEA MARKET
Marché Paul Bert, 93400 Saint-Ouen:
Bachelier Antiquités, allée 1, stand 17.
Tel: 01 40 11 89 98.
Michel Morin, allée 1, stand 20.
Tel: 01 40 11 19

LA TUILE À LOUP
35 rue Daubenton, 75005 Paris.
Tel: 01 47 07 28 90
Contemporary pottery, baskets. Literature on rural
life by Chabrol, Hélias, Mistral and Pourrat

MAISON DE LA LOZERE
1 bis rue Hautefeuille, 75006 Paris.
Tel: 01 43 26 93 99
and at 4 rue des Anges, Mende, Lozère
Furniture and contemporary woodcraft

REGIONS

ANTIQUITÉ BROCANTE
Catherine Ginioux, 10 rue des Forgerons,
15000 Aurillac. Tel: 04 71 48 27 76
Country objects

ANTIQUITÉS LE MAGE
61290 Longny-au-Perche. Tel: 02 33 25 66 88
Several floors of a village house stocked with
pottery, furniture, household linen, bedcovers
and a large range of traditional textiles

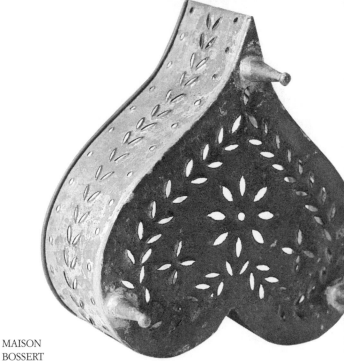

MAISON
BOSSERT
11 bis quai de Turckheim,
67000 Strasbourg.
Tel: 03 88 32 28 47
Textiles, ribbons and kelsh (mattress ticking from
Alsace), all made in the traditional way

PFIRSCH
20 rue de la Nuée Bleue, 67000 Strasbourg.
Tel: 03 88 32 72 73
Antiques

SOULEIADO
39 rue Proudhon, 13150 Tarascon, France.
Tel: 04 90 91 50 11
Provençal fabrics: orders accepted from the UK

UK

LONDON

ALFIES ANTIQUE MARKET
(Tues–Sat) 13–25 Church Street, Marylebone,
London NW8. Tel: 0171 723 6066
French country furniture, decorative objects

BAZAR
82 Golborne Road, London W10 5PS.
Tel: 0181 969 6262.
French country pieces, enamelware, painted
furniture, beds, mirrors

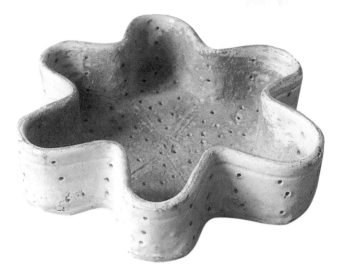

BRYONY THOMASSON
283 Westbourne Grove, Portobello Road,
London W11 (Sats).
Tel: 0171 731 3693 (for appointment on other days)
French rustic and handwoven textiles, tickings,
agricultural working clothes

CATHERINE NIMMO ANTIQUES
277 Lillie Road, London SW6 7LL.
Tel: 0171 385 2724
French furniture, objects, metalware, and
kitchenware (some 1940s and '50s pieces)

I. & J.L. BROWN
632–36 Kings Road, London SW6 2DU.
Tel: 0171 736 4141
French country furniture and pottery

IAN MANKIN
109 Regents Park Road, London NW1 8UR.
Tel: 0171 722 0997
and at 271 Wandsworth Bridge Road,
London SW6 2TX. Tel: 0171 371 8825
French tickings in many traditional colours

JUDY GREENWOOD
657 Fulham Road, London SW6 5PY.
Tel: 0171 736 6037
French beds, furniture, quilts, textiles, objects

NICOLE FABRE
592 Kings Road, London SW6 2DX.
Tel: 0171 384 3112
Antique French provincial furniture and textiles

SUMMERILL & BISHOP
100 Portland Road, London W11 4LN.
Tel: 0171 221 4566
Old French glass and enamelware, bistro glasses,
confit pots, storage jars, baskets

NUMBER 12
12 Cale Street, Chelsea Green,
London SW3 3QU. Tel: 0171 581 5022
and L'ENCOIGNURE
517 Kings Road, London SW10 0TX.
Tel: 0171 351 6465
French provincial furniture, confit pots

REGIONS

DENZIL GRANT
Hubbards Corner, Felsham Road,
Bradfield St George, Suffolk, IP30 OAQ
(by appointment). Tel: 01449 736576
French 17th to 19th-century country furniture

JACOB AND HIS FIERY ANGEL
7 Middle Street, Padstow, Cornwall PL28 8BT.
Tel: 01841 532 130/186.
French country furniture, clocks, 'marriage domes',
enamelware and kitchenware

PAVILION TEXTILES/ANTIQUES
Freshford Hall, Freshford, Bath BA3 6EJ
(by appointment). Tel: 01225 722 522
Large stock of old French linen, tickings,
decorative antiques and folk art

VINCENT DANÉ
Petworth Antique Centre, East Street,
Petworth, West Sussex GU28.
Tel: 01798 342 073
Rustic French furniture and pottery

USA

ABC CARPET & HOME
888 Broadway, New York, NY 10003-1258.
Tel: 212 473 3000
Furniture, antiques, rugs, household ware

EVELYNE CONQUARET ANTIQUES
Showplace Square West,
550 15th Street,
San Francisco, CA 94103.
Tel: 415 552 6100

MADE IN FRANCE
2913 Ferndale, Houston, TX 70098.
Tel: 713 529 7049
Tableware

MAISON
148 South La Brea Ave,
Los Angeles, CA 90036.
Tel: 213 935 3157
French country household ware

LA MAISON DE NICOLE
66 E. Walton Street, Chicago, IL 60611.
Tel: 312 943 3988
French country household ware

MILLER & ARNEY ANTIQUES
1737 Wisconsin Ave NW, Washington DC 20007.
Tel: 202 338 2369

PIERRE DEUX FRENCH COUNTRY STORES
870 Madison Ave, New York, NY 10021.
Tel: 212 570 9343
and other major cities throughout the USA
Furniture, household accessories, tableware
and kitchenware

THE POTTERY BARN
2100 Chestnut Street, San Francisco, CA.
Tel: 415 441 1787
and other major cities throughout the USA
Tableware, household ware, furniture

RALF'S ANTIQUES
807 N. La Cienega Blvd, W. Hollywood,
CA 90069. Tel: 310 659 1966

TOM HAYES & ASSOCIATES
AND TOBY WEST LTD
Atlanta Decorative Arts Center, 351 Peachtree
Hills Avenue, NE Atlanta, GA 30305
Tel: 404 233 7425
Antiques

WILLIAMS-SONOMA
150 Post Street, San Francisco, CA 94108.
Tel: 415 362 6904
and other major cities throughout the USA
Kitchenware, tableware and linens

AUSTRALIA

HOWELL & HOWELL
84 Queen Street, Woollahra,
Sydney, NSW 2025.
Tel: 02 9328 1212
French 18th and 19th-century country furniture

THE COUNTRY TRADER
122 Oxford Street, Paddington, NSW 2021.
Tel: 02 9331 7809
French provincial antique and decorative furniture

PHOTOGRAPHIC CREDITS

Samuel Dhote 98, 99, 101 *left and right*, 102–3, 104 *below*, 105 *right*, 106–7, 109

Bernard-Marie Lauté 15, 44, 55 *left and right*, 56–57, 59, 60, 61, 62, 64, 65, 94 *below left*

Pierre Masclaux 9, 26 *below left*, 28 *left*, 29, 46–47, 49, 50–51, 52, 53, 78, 79

Pierre Soissons 1, 4–5, 6, 12–13, 18, 20, 21, 26 *above right,* 27 *top and bottom left,*
33 *above*, 34, 35, 37, 38, 39, 40, 41, 82 *above*, 90, 104 *above*

Ivan Terestchenko 2, 3, 17, 32 *left*, 33 *centre*, 54, 68, 70, 71, 72–73, 74, 75 *above and below,*
76–77, 85 *right above and below*, 93, 94 *above left*, 95 *right*, 96, 97

All these photographs, with the exception of those taken by Bernard-Marie Lauté,
were taken in collaboration with the author between 1995 and 1996

Other photographers contributing to this book are as follows:

Marie-France Boyer 10 *above and below left*, 16, 22, 26 *above left*,
28 *right*, 36, 58 *above and below left*, 63, 66–67, 82 *below*, 87, 88, 89,
94 *above right*, 95 *above and below*, 105 *left*

Sara Boyer-Durin 107 *right*

Bernard et Catherine Desjeux 30–31, 80–81

Jacques Dirand/The World of Interiors 83, 84, 86

Alexis Forestier 27 *centre left*

Guillaume de Laubier/The World of Interiors 10 *below right*, 23, 24–25

Christophe Soubigou 94 *below right*

Claude Weber 26 *below right*, 27 *centre right*, 58 *centre,* 108, 112

In addition, most of the objects illustrated in the book under the heading
'Everyday Objects' were photographed especially for this book by
Claude Weber and Ivan Terestchenko

THE AUTHOR WISHES TO THANK

Jean-Jacques Breton, Vincent Dané,
Dominique Dufayet, Olivier Durin, Claude et Alain Fassier,
Isabelle Forestier, Marie-France et Michel Joblin,
Martyn et Yves Levesque, la Maison de la Mariée, le Musée du Vieux-Nîmes,
Roger Penland, Béatrice Saalburg, Dhaliette Suchère,
Jean Tucoo-Chalat, Valentin Vincendet,
The World of Interiors

The author wishes to express special thanks
to La Tuile à Loup and Cuisinophilie in Paris, and
Antiquités Le Mage (Perche) for lending most
of the objects photographed for this book